"I loose the world
from all I thought it was."
ACIM, W-132

Holy Spirit
PRAYERS FOR SURRENDER
The Rose Book

Cate Grieves

All quotes are from *A Course in Miracles* (ACIM), copyright ©1992, 1999, 2007 by the Foundation for Inner Peace, 448 Ignacio Blvd., #306, Novato, CA 94949, www.acim.org and info@acim.org, used with permission.

We would like to express gratitude for the Foundation for Inner Peace.

This is a key for the quote references:
T = Text
W = Workbook for Students
M = Manual for Teachers
C = Clarification of Terms
S = The Song of Prayer Pamphlet
P = Psychotherapy Pamphlet

Designed by: Shannon Williams
Cover and interior photography: Unsplash.com

First Edition: March 2023

Blessings, Friend

Welcome, my beautiful brother. I welcome you to these Holy Spirit Prayers that help foster an attitude of surrendering ourselves to the Love of God. Each prayer has been divinely gifted from the Holy Spirit to help our mind align with the decision to "be still" and "let go of everything we think we know". The prayers and the quotes work powerfully together, as you read them slowly, to shift your mind into an experience of peace, love and joy. The prayers and quotes have the elements of inviting the Holy Spirit in, asking for His help and feeling ourselves surrendering to Him. The Holy Spirit's perception is the miracle that brings forth the wisdom and peace that replaces the false beliefs we made up ourselves. Please read each prayer slowly and stay with each prayer and quote in quiet and silence. Feel yourself willing to let the words wash over you and be the prayer of your heart.

Love,
Cate

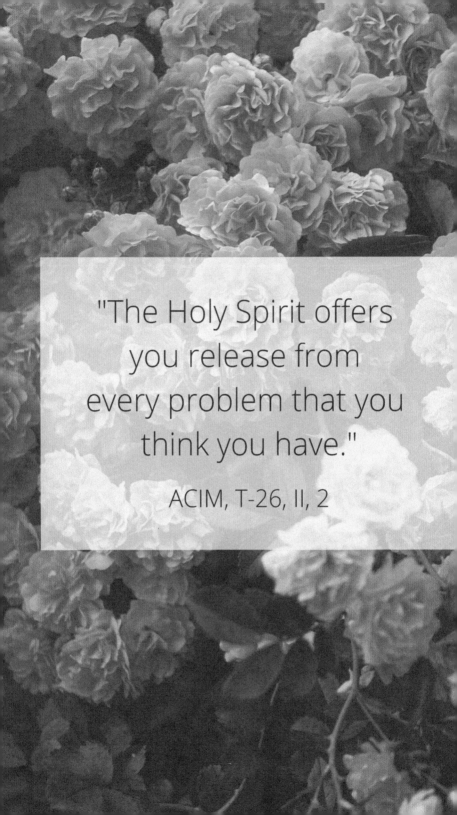

"The Holy Spirit offers you release from every problem that you think you have."

ACIM, T-26, II, 2

Holy Spirit

Be You in charge

I give You my life,

My body and my mind

I offer it to You to use

However you choose

Let me be the instrument of

Thy Peace

Thy Love

Thy Wisdom

Amen

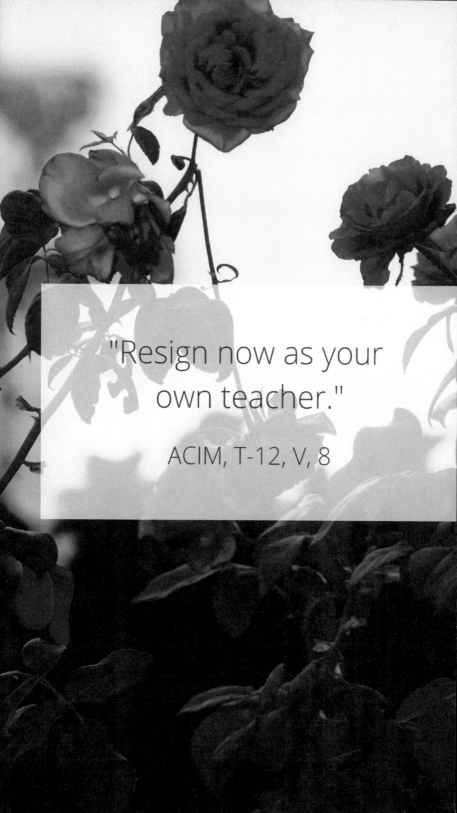

"Resign now as your own teacher."

ACIM, T-12, V, 8

Holy Spirit

I am tired of my ego mind

I want Your Mind instead

I want only Your Mind

I want only Your Thoughts

Your Thoughts are always loving and kind

They don't distort Reality

They see only my Christ Brother

Shining before me

Shining in everlasting light

Let me only see my brother as he really is

Let me only see as You do

And I will remain

In Eternal happiness

Amen

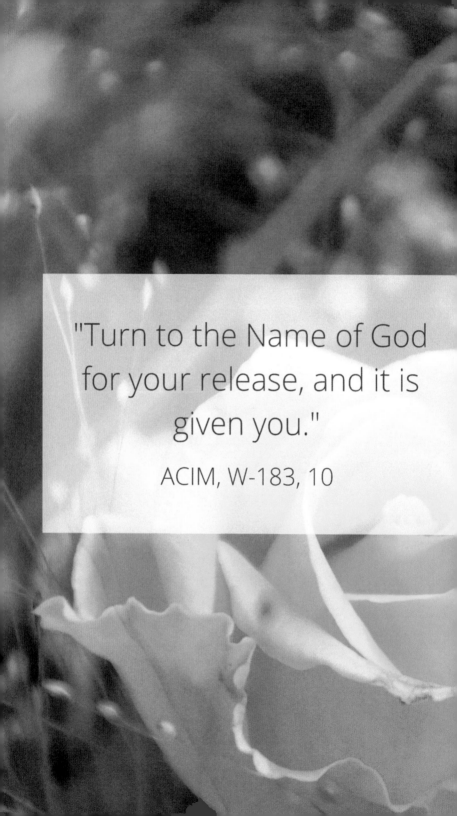

"Turn to the Name of God for your release, and it is given you."

ACIM, W-183, 10

Holy Spirit

I surrender to Your true perception

I surrender to God's Thoughts

His Thought holds me as a star

Unchangeable in an eternal sky

So high in Heaven, am I set

That those outside of Heaven

Know not that I am there

Yet still and pure and lovely

Will I shine through all eternity

There was no time

I was not there

No instant did I grow dimmer

Or less perfect

Amen

"Your past is what you have taught yourself. Let it all go."

ACIM, W-195

My brother's past is mine

I wish to be free of all the past

I will to share in this release today

And release all grievances for you to undo

Please help me let no dark clouds of my past

Obscure him from Your truth

And let me seek

Only what I can find of him

Here in the present

Let me seek now

Where it is

And let it dawn on my eyes

His beauty and loveliness

As it is

Amen

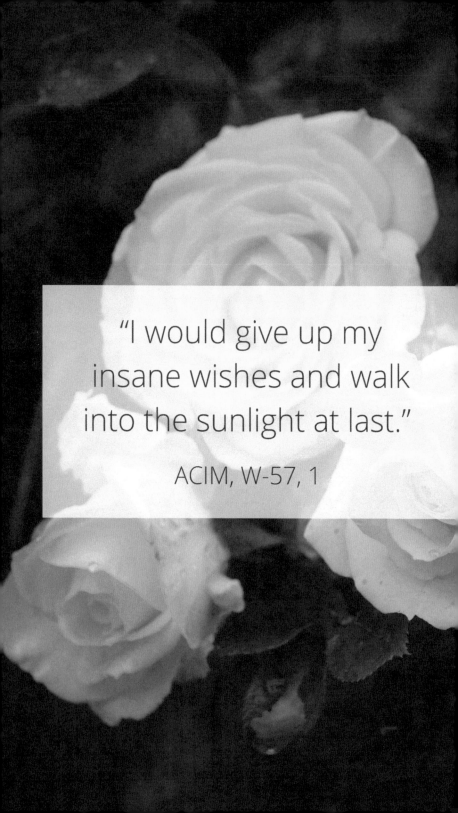

"I would give up my insane wishes and walk into the sunlight at last."

ACIM, W-57, 1

Holy Spirit

Please be the shining light

That assists me on my journey Home

To a place I never left

Thoughts seem to come and go

And yet I am not always aware of them

But I will to notice them

So that I can give them to You

Please take any insane thoughts

I cast them onto thee

Please bring the quiet thoughts

That God thinks with me

To my holy mind

Amen

"Give up the world!
But not to sacrifice.
You never wanted it."

ACIM, T-30, V, 9

HOLY SPIRIT

I come to You

On bended knee

I ask You to guide me

Today as You always do

I am in my wrong mind

And choosing from insane thoughts

I am choosing the wrong voice

To listen to

Help me choose again

Help me remember to stop

And actively choose Your way

Amen

"Step back from fear, and make advance to love."

ACIM, W-196, 11

Holy Spirit

Please lead me

I step back so You can be in charge

You know the way

I do not

You will never keep from me

What You would have me learn

And so I trust in You today

To communicate to me

All that You know

And all that I need to learn

Please decide for me today

As I trust in You

To guide me

Amen

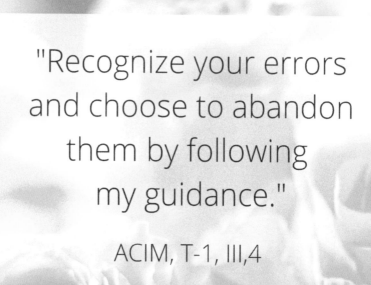

"Recognize your errors
and choose to abandon
them by following
my guidance."

ACIM, T-1, III,4

Holy Spirit

You are the love that surrounds me

The love that lifts me up

The love that smiles my smile

Please shine on me today

Be the mind that I choose all my thoughts from

Your thoughts only see the divine in all

Your thoughts have no worry or anxiety

They are perfectly calm and content

know that all choices that come from Your thoughts

Are the miracle for all minds

I trust today

That following Your guidance

Always brings about the healing of my mind

And with that healing are all minds healed

Amen

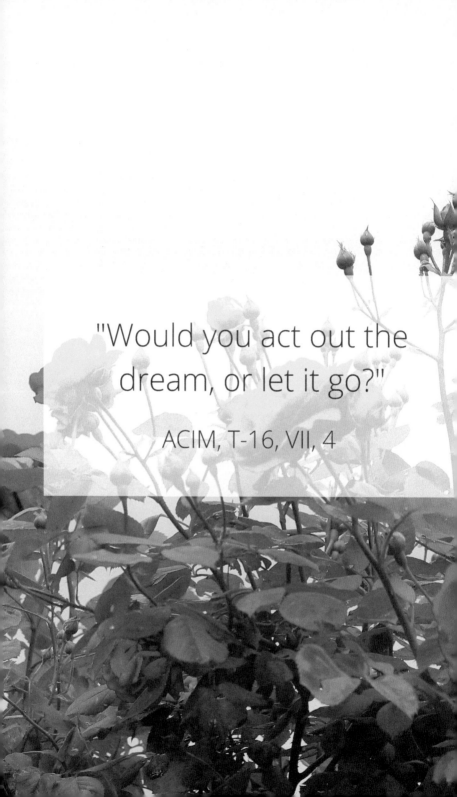

"Would you act out the
dream, or let it go?"

ACIM, T-16, VII, 4

Holy Spirit

You serve a mighty purpose

To correct all specialness

In my mind

So that I will abide

In the Christ that I am

Which inhabits not a body

But a holy Mind instead

Please help me understand that

What is within

Cannot be outside

And that I could never be apart

From what is at the very center

Of my Life

Amen

"Let go all the trivial things that churn and bubble on the surface of your mind, and reach down and below them to the Kingdom of Heaven."

ACIM, W-47, 7

Dear Holy Spirit

My only desire is to awaken

To the truth of my Identity

Of the Holy Christ that I am

A wholly loving Son

Of a Father so Loving

A Father that has never condemned

But just loved and loved

And loved me into infinity

Amen

"This is the way salvation works. As you step back, the light in you steps forward and encompasses the world."

ACIM, W-156, 6

Holy Spirit

Speak through me today

Speak your wise wisdom

Smile your loving smile through me

Hug through me

Kiss through me

Share through me

I give myself to You today

Use me to share Your unbounded Love

Amen

"Let every voice but God's be still in me."

ACIM, W-254

Deepest Gratitude today

For all that You give me

I surrender to Your loving ways

Your kindness

Your caring

You love me as the perfect Child of God that I am

You see no differences or separation

You see only the same

The same perfection

Everywhere

Always

And I am that

I am that Love

Blessings to You today Holy Spirit

As I join You in Your Love of me

Amen

"Is it a sacrifice to give up nothing, and to receive the Love of God forever?"

ACIM, T-24, II, 6

Holy Spirit

I have taught myself badly

I have believed many thoughts

That are not true

I am ready to give them up

They serve no purpose

But to keep me bound

To a mind of judgment

I wish to be free

I desire only the Peace of God

So please be in charge today

Amen

"Release is given you the instant you desire it."

ACIM, T-18, VII, 4

Holy Spirit

I surrender

I give you my mind and heart

Please bring me the wisdom that is Yours

I want the Peace of God

I want it above all else

I am entitled to miracles

I am entitled to shifts from fear to Love

The Love of God

That will replace my thoughts of fear

Thank you and I love you

Amen

"Today I lay aside all sick illusions of myself, and let my Father tell me Who I really am."

ACIM, W-120, 2

Holy Spirit

Help me realize

That Christ abides within

In the part of me that

Shares my Father's Will

Please help me

Experience my Christ identity

Please make Oneness clear to me

I desire only this

I surrender my will

And allow this most beautiful experience

To be shown to me

Amen

"Release yourself to Him
Whose function is release."

ACIM,T-18, IV, 6

HOLY SPIRIT

You are the perfect bridge

To carry me home

Carry me on your shoulders

Lift me up when I can't move

I will rest and let you shift me

Move me with your brilliance

Shine in me your eternal light

In me, as me

Drop me at God's feet

And leave me there to grow

To unwind to the glorious glory

And be held by the wondrous view

Of the never-ending shining love

Amen

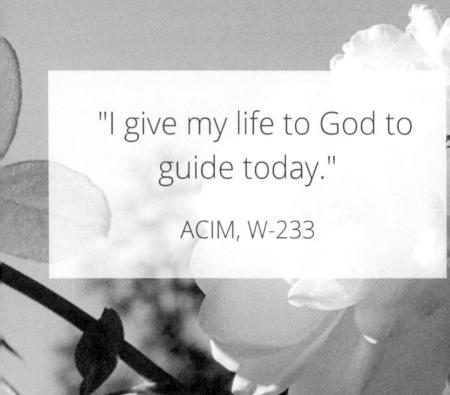

"I give my life to God to guide today."

ACIM, W-233

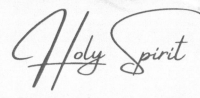

Holy Spirit

God's Thoughts shine forever

They wait only for my welcome

And remembering

I ask for them today

To replace what has no use

I welcome God's Thoughts today

I welcome Your clear guidance today

I wish for You to think for me

So that I can rest

And know that You will answer

And respond for me today

Amen

"I do not know what anything is for."

ACIM, W-233

Holy Spirit

Be You in charge

Use my arms, legs and tongue today

To speak Your love and wisdom

Allow Your love to extend to all around

I have no idea about where, how and when

But ask that You be the mind that directs me today

I love you and I join you

Amen

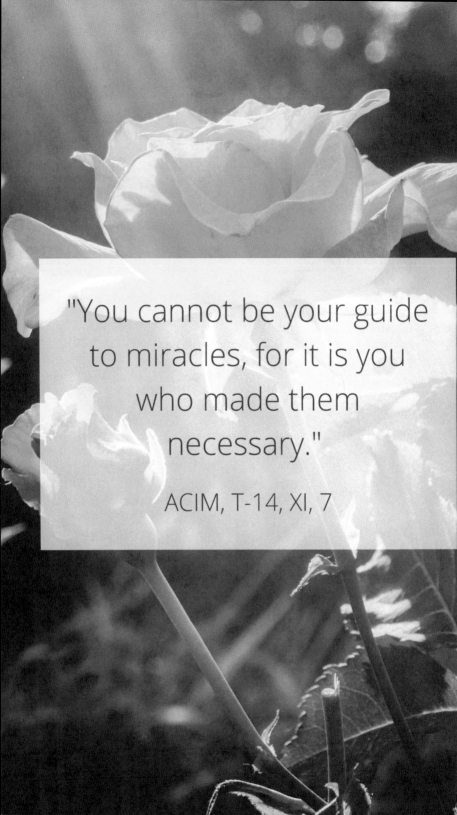

"You cannot be your guide to miracles, for it is you who made them necessary."

ACIM, T-14, XI, 7

HOLY SPIRIT

The miracle undoes what never was

I thought it was something

But You show me that it wasn't what I thought

I can be affected only by my thoughts

So I ask that you remove

All thoughts that are not in accord

With Your Thoughts

Of love, life and joy

I give you all my thoughts today

That are fear based

Please show me a way to see this differently

Amen

"Let me be still and listen
to the truth."

ACIM, W-106

Holy Spirit

I am still

I lay aside all thoughts and all concepts

I lay aside all images I hold about myself

I empty my mind of everything

I think is true or false

I empty my mind of everything

I think is good or bad

I let go of thoughts that judge myself or others

As worthy or shameful

I hold onto nothing

I bring no thought from the past

I bring no belief I have ever learned

I let it all go

I forget this world

I forget this course

I stand here surrendered

I come now to you God

With empty hands

Amen

"Forget this world, forget this course, and come with wholly empty hands unto your God."

ACIM, W-189, 7

HOLY SPIRIT

I choose to sit with an empty mind

Empty of future and past thoughts

Just sitting with pure Divine Love

Right here and now

I choose You, Holy Spirit

You are my right mind

I choose Your Peace

I choose Your Joy and Happiness

In this Holy Instant, Now

Amen

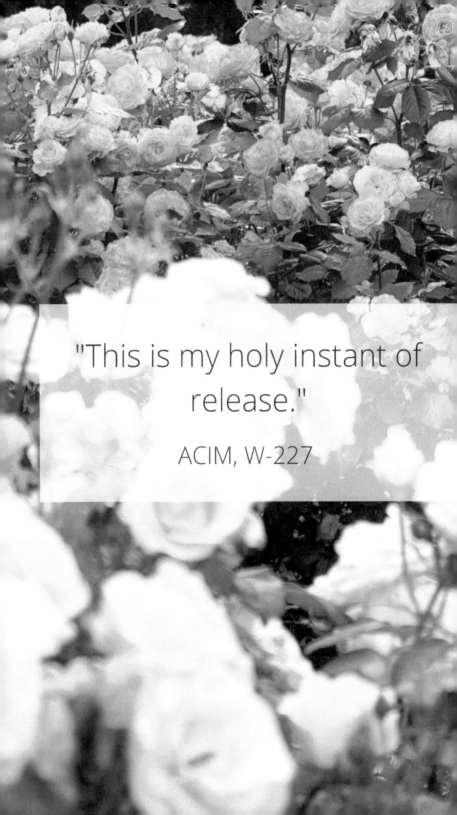

"This is my holy instant of release."

ACIM, W-227

HOLY SPIRIT

In the stillness of today

I surrender my will

And I say to You

I will to do it

And let You illuminate

My holy thoughts

Upon my holy altar

And shower me with Holy Gifts

Of God's Glory and Adoring Love

Amen

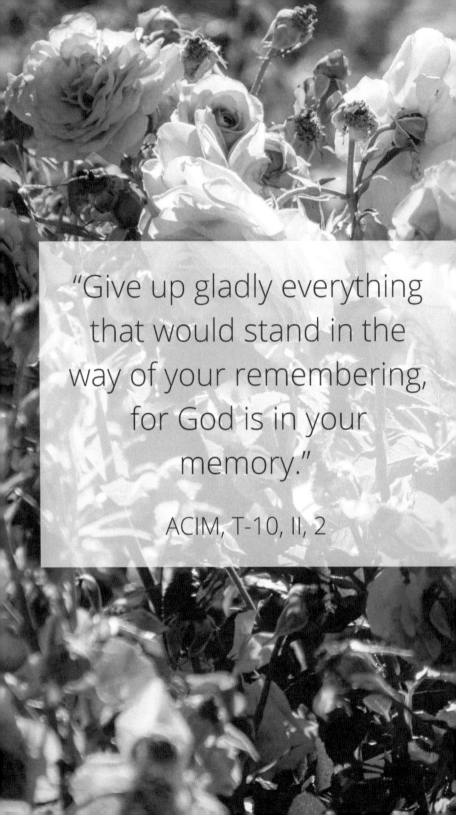

"Give up gladly everything that would stand in the way of your remembering, for God is in your memory."

ACIM, T-10, II, 2

Holy Spirit

I accept the Atonement for myself

This is my only commitment

To have You correct all error

And bring the truth into my Mind

The holy Mind I share with God

One with Him forever

Please show me what is left to release

As my one desire is to only know

Myself as God created me

Amen

"Creation leans across the bars of time to lift the heavy burden from the world. Lift up your hearts to greet its advent."

ACIM, S-3, IV, 9

Holy Spirit

Please be in charge of time

Help me see time differently

Help me see it as you do

I am still breaking time

Into past, present and future

For my own purposes

I anticipate the future

Based on my past

And plan accordingly

Which doesn't allow the miracle

Which will intervene between them

Free me to be born again

In a timeless changeless Reality

Of your Mind of Love

Amen

"Pause and be still a little while, and see how far you rise above the world, when you release your mind from chains and let it seek the level where it finds itself at home."

ACIM, W-128, 6

HOLY SPIRIT

I will stop thinking in this moment

I allow everything to be as it is

I allow all characters to play their part

I am not responsible for their lives

I am not responsible for making them happy

I am not responsible for their quality of life

I am not responsible for anything that they experience

They are responsible for choosing either fear or love

I cannot make that choice for them

I can only make my own choice

Which is to allow You

To choose for me

Amen

"In the Name of God,
be wholly willing to
abandon all illusions "

ACIM, T-16, IV, 9

Holy Spirit

Please help me see how I am projecting

By making an outside picture

From an inward condition

I wish to realize how I am doing this

So that I am released from this bondage

Please illuminate how this occurs

So that I can start to become

The observer of my thoughts

And start to see that they are not mine

But a constant stream of nothingness

Made to look like something

I put You in charge today

So that the miracle comes

Shining into my mind

Amen

Dearest Brother, we offer you this christ blessing

I love you
I bless you
I honor you

You are guiltless
You are innocent
You are sinless

You are perfect
You are whole
You are complete

You are the Holy Christ
Your worth is established by God

Love,

Cate & Shannon

About the Author

anuary 2015, after a two-year deep immersion with the teachings of A Course in acles and joining with the Holy Spirit and Jesus to undo the split mind, Cate's mind kened to the infinite, vast, eternal, boundless, all-encompassing Love that is. In that ment, a download of understanding of the Course's teachings entered her mind a knowing became clear that "God is in everything I see because God is in my d". Cate's mind entered the Song of Heaven, where perfect Oneness sang the most utiful song of love and gratitude.

New Years Day 2016, the Holy Spirit showed Cate a picture of the cover of a Holy it prayer book and guided her to start writing these prayers down. Over time, the ers were divided by themes from A Course in Miracles and a flower background gn was given for easy recognition to the theme. These prayer books are here to be pful for any mind that wishes to know how to "pray". Forgiveness prayer is to invite Hoy Spirit in, ask Him for help to see our brother or the situation differently and า wait for His beautiful loving answer to enter our mind.

Holy Spirit's purpose for these prayers, is to "Let these prayers nourish the desert he unawakened mind with the living waters of God's Love".

To find out more about Cate, visit: categrieves.com

About the Designer

ecember of 2020, Shannon was guided to support Cate in all things. This book is of the many ways she is so honored to serve and it has been a beautifully divine erience playing her part in following guidance on the design of this prayer book. nnon is filled with gratitude to be of service to Him, to Cate and to all of her hers to be truly helpful in all ways.

nnon has been A Course in Miracles student since 2009 and joined with Jesus kly to learn his Course. After two years of practicing ACIM and relying on Jesus to le her, bringing in miracles, shifting her perception from fear to love, Shannon was ed outside of time and space. She realized that where she was, is what she is. She erienced freedom from everything she once believed and it continues to bring the erience of beauty, in every moment.

To find out more about Shannon, visit: thehappylearners.com

Made in the USA
Middletown, DE
27 January 2024

48649229R00035